MASTERING RETIREMENT

RETIREMENT SOLUTIONS GROUP

RETIREMENT
SOLUTIONS
GROUP

REVISED EDITION

MASTERING
RETIREMENT

THE COMPLETE MANUAL TO PLAN AND PREPARE FOR A SAFE AND PROSPEROUS RETIREMENT

**RETIREMENT
SOLUTIONS GROUP**
EDUCATIONAL PUBLISHING

For Stacey

CONTENTS

Introduction: Charting Your Course

Bill's Journey to a Secure Retirement

Bill had always been a diligent saver. From the moment he received his first paycheck in his early twenties, he understood the importance of setting aside money for the future. As a young man, Bill watched his parents struggle financially during retirement. They had worked hard their entire lives but were caught off guard by unexpected medical expenses and the rising cost of living. Determined not to repeat their mistakes, Bill committed to saving regularly, even when it meant sacrificing some luxuries along the way.

As Bill progressed in his career, he took advantage of every opportunity to grow his nest egg. He contributed diligently to his 401(k), taking full advantage of employer matching. He also opened an IRA and invested in a diversified portfolio that included stocks, bonds, and mutual funds. Over the years, Bill educated himself on the basics of investing, following market trends and adjusting his strategy as needed. He wasn't looking to strike it rich overnight—his goal was simple: to build a solid financial foundation that would support him and his wife, Susan, throughout their retirement.

By the time Bill turned 60, he felt confident in his financial future. He had amassed a substantial portfolio, and with retirement just around the corner, he was looking forward to enjoying the fruits of his labor. Bill and Susan had plans to travel, spend more time with their grandchildren, and finally take up those hobbies they had always put off—Bill with his woodworking, and Susan with her gardening.

However, as Bill's retirement date approached, the financial world began to show signs of trouble. It was 2007, and although the market had been on a steady upward climb, there were murmurs of an impending crisis. Bill noticed the housing market starting to wobble, and he recalled the stories his father used to tell about the Great Depression. It made him uneasy, but like many others, he wasn't sure if these were just minor tremors or the sign of something bigger.

In the summer of 2008, the tremors turned into an earthquake. The collapse of Lehman Brothers and the subsequent financial meltdown sent shockwaves across global markets. Bill watched in disbelief as his carefully built portfolio began to nosedive. Stocks that had once been reliable were now losing value at an alarming rate, and the 24-hour news cycle did nothing to ease his anxiety. He had seen market downturns before, but this felt different—it felt personal.

Bill was faced with a critical decision: should he stay the course or cut his losses? The fear was palpable, not just in the markets but in his own home. Susan, who had always trusted Bill's judgment when it came to finances, began to voice her concerns. They had worked too hard to lose everything now. Friends and neighbors were panicking, selling off their investments, and retreating to the perceived safety of cash. The temptation to do the same was strong.

But Bill had prepared for this moment. Years earlier, he had worked closely with a financial advisor who specialized in retirement planning. Together, they had created a diversified portfolio designed to withstand market volatility. His advisor had emphasized the importance of not putting all his eggs in one basket. Bill's portfolio included a mix of equities, bonds, and fixed-income assets, as well as a cash reserve that was specifically set aside for emergencies.

More importantly, Bill had learned the value of patience. His advisor had walked him through various scenarios, including severe market downturns, and had explained the importance of staying the course. They had built a plan that didn't rely on timing the market but instead focused on long-term growth and preservation of capital. Bill knew that the worst thing he could do was to make impulsive decisions based on fear.

So, instead of following the herd, Bill and his advisor reviewed his financial plan. They made a few adjustments—reallocating some of his stock holdings into more conservative investments and slightly reducing their planned withdrawals to ensure his cash reserves would last longer if needed. They also took advantage of the market downturn by reinvesting in undervalued assets that were likely to recover over time. Bill understood that while the market was down now, it wouldn't stay that way forever.

The years that followed were not easy. The market continued to fluctuate, and the recovery was slow. But Bill's disciplined approach paid off. By 2010, as the market began to rebound, Bill's portfolio was on the mend. He hadn't regained all of his losses, but his financial plan had done what it was supposed to—it had protected his lifestyle and preserved his capital. Bill and Susan were able to maintain their standard of living without making drastic changes. They still took that trip to Italy they had always dreamed of, and Bill spent his afternoons in his workshop, crafting beautiful pieces of furniture for his family.

As time passed, Bill reflected on what had happened and what he had learned. He realized that his success wasn't due to luck—it was the result of years of careful planning, educating himself, and working with a knowledgeable advisor who understood the unique challenges of retirement. Bill's story is a testament to the power of strategic retirement planning. He didn't panic during the storm; he stayed the course, confident in the knowledge that his plan was built to weather even the fiercest financial tempests.

Today, Bill enjoys his retirement with a deep sense of security and peace of mind. He's confident that the choices he made were the right ones, and he knows his financial plan will continue to support him and Susan for the rest of their lives. Bill is also proud to pass on the lessons he's learned to his children and grandchildren, hoping to inspire them to take control of their financial futures with the same care and foresight.

As you embark on your journey to secure your financial future, it's important to remember that the most successful plans are those tailored to your unique needs. To help you craft a strategy that aligns perfectly with your goals, we invite you to book a complimentary **Retirement Mastery Consultation**. In this one-on-one session, you'll receive personalized insights and actionable steps to ensure your retirement plan is both robust and adaptable.

The Importance of Strategic Retirement Planning

Bill's story is a powerful reminder of what's at stake in retirement planning. Just like Bill, you've worked hard and saved diligently to reach this stage of your life. But achieving a secure and fulfilling retirement requires more than just accumulating savings—it demands careful planning, a deep understanding of financial markets, and the ability to adapt to changing economic conditions.

The financial landscape today is more complex and interconnected than ever before. Market trends can shift rapidly, influenced by global events, government policies, technological advancements, and even social changes. These trends directly impact your retirement savings and income, making it crucial to stay informed and proactive in managing your finances.

Strategic retirement planning is about more than just accumulating wealth. It's about protecting what you've earned, ensuring that your money lasts as long as you do, and making decisions that align with your personal goals and values. By understanding market trends and how they influence your retirement plan, you can avoid common pitfalls, minimize risks, and seize opportunities that enhance your financial security.

Consider the alternative: entering retirement without a plan, or with a plan that doesn't account for market volatility, inflation, or changes in your personal situation. The result could be financial stress, reduced lifestyle choices, or even the fear of outliving your savings. But with a strategic approach, you can navigate these challenges with confidence, knowing that your retirement is built on a solid foundation.

What You'll Learn

This book is your guide to mastering retirement in an ever-changing financial world. Whether you're just starting to plan your retirement or are already retired and looking to optimize your strategy, this resource is designed to provide you with the knowledge and tools you need to secure your financial future.

Here's what you'll learn:

- **Understanding the Financial Landscape**: We'll explore how past and present market trends impact your retirement and how you can use this knowledge to make smarter investment decisions.
- **Strategic Insights for Retirement Planning**: Discover how to balance growth with stability, adapt to market changes, and protect your capital as you transition from saving to spending in retirement.
- **Taxes in Retirement**: Learn about critical tax considerations, including Roth conversions and Required Minimum Distributions (RMDs), that can significantly affect your retirement income.

- **Insurance Planning**: Understand the role of various insurance products—term life, whole life, and disability insurance—in safeguarding your retirement and ensuring peace of mind.
- **Key Ages and Milestones**: We'll outline the critical ages for decisions like when to claim Social Security, when RMDs begin, and how these milestones affect your retirement planning.
- **Managing Cash Flow in Retirement**: Get practical advice on budgeting, creating reliable income streams, and managing debt to ensure you have the cash flow needed to enjoy your retirement fully.
- **Smart Investment Options**: Explore different investment vehicles, including annuities, indexed accounts, and structured notes, to find the right mix for your retirement portfolio.
- **Crafting Your Financial Legacy**: Learn how to leave a lasting impact through effective estate planning, charitable giving, and ensuring your financial legacy for future generations.

Throughout this journey, we'll emphasize the importance of being proactive, staying informed, and seeking professional advice when needed. Your retirement is a time to enjoy life, not to worry about finances. With the right strategies, you can navigate market trends, protect your wealth, and secure a future that aligns with your dreams.

So, are you ready to chart your course toward a secure and prosperous retirement? Let's begin this journey together.

Download The Workbook

Take control of your retirement planning with our comprehensive workbook. Filled with exercises, reflections, and action steps, this guide will help you turn your retirement dreams into reality.

Benefits of the Workbook:

- Gain a clear understanding of the financial landscape.
- Learn how to protect your savings against market volatility.
- Develop a personalized retirement plan aligned with your goals.
- Prepare for productive discussions with your financial planner.

Scan or visit the link below to download your free copy now:

MASTERRETIREMENT.TODAY/WORKBOOK

Mastering Retirement

Disclaimer

The content in this book is intended for informational and educational purposes only and should not be construed as financial, legal, or tax advice. The strategies, tips, and recommendations presented are based on general retirement planning principles and may not be suitable for every individual. Before making any financial decisions, consult a licensed financial advisor, tax professional, or legal expert who can assess your unique situation and provide personalized advice.

The authors and publishers of this book make no guarantees about the accuracy, completeness, or applicability of the information contained herein. Any action you take based on the content in this book is at your own risk. Market conditions, tax laws, and financial regulations may change over time, and individual financial situations vary, so it is essential to seek professional guidance before implementing any investment or retirement strategy.

By reading this book you acknowledge that the authors, publishers, and any associated parties are not responsible for any financial losses, damages, or liabilities that may arise from your use of the information provided.

CHAPTER 1

Understanding the Financial Landscape

When planning for retirement, it's crucial to understand how the financial markets behave and how external forces, like government policies or global events, can shape the economy. By grasping the broader economic context, you can better anticipate market shifts and position your retirement portfolio to withstand fluctuations.

The Evolution of Market Trends: Learning from the Past

The financial market has always experienced cycles of growth and contraction. From the tech boom of the 1990s to the 2008 financial crisis, these periods of prosperity and downturn have left profound impacts on investors, particularly retirees. Understanding these market cycles can help you better prepare for the future.

The Roaring '90s: Tech Boom and Economic Growth

The 1990s were marked by rapid technological advancements and the birth of the internet age. This era saw unprecedented growth in stock markets, driven primarily by tech companies. Investors who put money into companies like Microsoft and Apple saw their portfolios skyrocket, leading many to believe the market would keep growing indefinitely.

Application for You: Imagine you were about to retire in 1999, after a decade of phenomenal growth. You might have been tempted to keep a large portion of your portfolio in high-growth tech stocks, hoping for continued gains. However, markets are cyclical, and what followed was the **dot-com bubble burst** in 2000, where many tech stocks lost nearly all their value. This downturn would have been devastating if your portfolio was heavily invested in tech without a diversified approach.

Lesson: Avoiding over-reliance on one sector is key. Even during strong markets, diversify your portfolio across different asset classes (stocks, bonds, cash) and industries to avoid large losses when the cycle turns.

The Dot-Com Bubble and 9/11: Sudden Volatility

By 2000, the dot-com bubble burst, and many companies that had soared in value suddenly collapsed. Investors who hadn't anticipated the downturn lost significant portions of their savings. Just when the market was beginning to recover, the tragic events of September 11, 2001, sent further shock-waves through the global economy. Both the dot-com bust and the 9/11 attacks led to increased volatility and fear in the markets.

Example: Take Janet, a retiree who had been enjoying substantial returns during the tech boom. By late 2000, her portfolio had lost nearly 30% of its value. However, because she had planned for downturns, she had allocated 40% of her portfolio to bonds and cash, which held up during the market crash. This helped her avoid having to sell off stocks at the worst time.

Application for You: Market downturns often catch people by surprise. You might be preparing for retirement during what feels like a stable period, but unexpected events (like 9/11 or another recession) can lead to a sharp decline in your savings. Diversify your investments and include stable, less volatile assets like bonds and cash to protect your wealth.

The 2008 Financial Crisis: A Global Economic Collapse

The 2008 financial crisis was one of the most dramatic market collapses in recent history. What began as a housing bubble burst in the U.S. turned into a global financial meltdown. Stocks plummeted, and many individuals saw their retirement savings evaporate seemingly overnight. For those close to retirement, this was especially frightening.

Example: Consider Tom and Mary, who were nearing retirement in 2007. At the time, their portfolio was heavily weighted in equities (about 80%). They hadn't revisited their investment plan in years, and when the market crashed in 2008, they saw their savings drop by nearly 40%. Suddenly, retirement no longer seemed possible. Fortunately, their financial advisor stepped in and helped them re-balance their portfolio, moving more into bonds, and they adjusted their retirement timeline by a couple of years to recover.

Lesson: As you approach retirement, gradually reduce your exposure to stocks and shift more towards bonds and other lower-risk assets. This will protect your savings from drastic losses right when you need them most.

Current Market Dynamics: A New Era of Complexity
Today, we're living in a more interconnected, technology-driven world, and the markets reflect that. Economic events in one part of

the world can impact your portfolio overnight. Government policies like interest rate changes, trade agreements, and monetary stimulus can have profound effects on the economy and retirement portfolios.

Global Events and Market Volatility

With globalization, markets now move quickly based on global news. Events like trade wars, pandemics, or geopolitical tensions can cause markets to rise or fall dramatically. For example, the COVID-19 pandemic led to a swift market crash in early 2020, but it was followed by an equally rapid recovery, spurred by government intervention and stimulus measures.

Application for You: Stay informed. Keeping an eye on global trends can help you anticipate short-term volatility and adjust your portfolio if necessary. However, it's important not to react to every headline. Instead, focus on long-term planning, with periodic adjustments based on your overall risk tolerance and financial goals.

Actionable Tip: Schedule annual portfolio reviews with your financial advisor. This ensures your investment strategy evolves as market conditions change, without making reactionary moves based on daily news.

Government Policies: The Impact of Interest Rates and Stimulus

Government interventions, such as interest rate cuts or increases, directly affect your retirement. Lower interest rates, for instance, can benefit borrowers but hurt retirees who rely on bond income. On the flip side, higher rates might help savers but can slow economic growth.

Example: During the post-2008 recovery, the Federal Reserve kept interest rates at historically low levels to stimulate the economy. While this helped businesses grow and the stock market recover, it left retirees who had relied on bond income in a bind. Low bond yields meant less interest income, forcing many to look for alternative income sources or adjust their lifestyle expectations.

Application for You: Diversify your sources of income. Don't rely solely on bond yields or stock dividends. Consider adding income-generating assets like annuities, real estate, or dividend-paying stocks to your portfolio. This will provide a broader base of income streams during retirement, helping you withstand changes in interest rates or market performance.

How to Use Market Trends to Your Advantage

Now that you understand how market cycles and external events affect your portfolio, here's how you can apply that knowledge to your retirement planning:

1. **Diversify Across Asset Classes and Sectors**:
   - As you've seen from past market crashes, having all your savings in one sector or asset class can be risky. Diversification is a key strategy to minimize risk while still participating in market growth.
   - **Example**: If you're heavily invested in technology, consider adding healthcare, utilities, or bonds to your portfolio. This spreads risk and ensures that if one sector falls, others might remain stable or grow.
2. **Adjust Your Portfolio as You Age**:
   - In your 30s and 40s, it makes sense to have more exposure to equities for long-term growth. But as you near retirement, reducing your risk exposure and adding

more stable assets (like bonds, indexed annuities, or cash reserves) will protect you from market downturns.

- ° **Actionable Step**: Begin shifting your portfolio allocation every 5-10 years as you approach retirement, reducing stock exposure by 10-20% and adding bonds or cash reserves.

3. **Stay Informed, But Don't Overreact**:
   - ° Pay attention to global trends and financial news, but avoid making knee-jerk reactions. If your retirement plan is well-constructed, it should account for periodic downturns.
   - ° **Example**: If you hear about a potential trade war that could affect the market, schedule a review with your advisor to discuss any adjustments, but avoid making decisions based on fear.

Conclusion: Building a Resilient Retirement Plan

Understanding the financial landscape is critical for building a resilient retirement plan. Market trends, government policies, and global events will always impact your investments, but with the right strategy, you can navigate these challenges confidently.

- **Action Step**: Start today by reviewing your portfolio. Are you diversified? Do you have enough safe assets to protect your retirement income from volatility? Meet with your advisor to make adjustments and create a strategy that accounts for both current market conditions and your long-term goals.

As you move forward in this book, we'll dive deeper into how to protect your capital, optimize taxes, and ensure your retirement plan is built to last. Now that you understand how markets work, let's explore the next crucial aspect of your financial future—preserving your wealth and making it last throughout your retirement.

CHAPTER 2

Strategic Insights for Retirement Planning

Retirement planning is about more than just building a nest egg; it's about ensuring that your savings last throughout your retirement years while maintaining the lifestyle you desire. As you transition from the accumulation phase (saving and investing) to the distribution phase (withdrawing and spending), your financial strategy needs to adapt. This chapter will guide you through the key strategies that can help you achieve a stable and secure retirement.

1. Balancing Growth with Stability

As you approach retirement, the way you think about investments should shift. During your working years, the focus is often on growth—maximizing returns to build your retirement savings. But as you near retirement, the focus shifts to preservation—ensuring that your savings are protected from market volatility while still generating enough growth to outpace inflation.

Growth vs. Stability: Finding the Right Mix

Example: Imagine you're 10 years away from retirement. You've been heavily invested in stocks, enjoying the growth they provide. However, as retirement nears, you start to feel uneasy about potential market downturns. If another 2008-style crash happens just before you retire, your savings could take a significant hit. This is where the balance between growth and stability becomes crucial.

Application for You:

- **Assess Your Risk Tolerance**: As retirement approaches, consider how much risk you're comfortable with. This typically decreases as you get closer to retirement.
  - ◦ **Action Step**: Use a risk tolerance questionnaire, available through most financial advisors or online, to evaluate your comfort level with various types of investments. This will guide your asset allocation decisions.
- **Adjust Your Asset Allocation**: Gradually shift from a portfolio dominated by equities to one that includes more bonds, cash, and other lower-risk assets.
  - ◦ **Example**: If your portfolio is currently 80% stocks and 20% bonds, consider gradually shifting to a 60/40 or even 50/50 mix as you approach retirement.
  - ◦ **Action Step**: Meet with your financial advisor to create a timeline for adjusting your asset allocation. This might involve rebalancing your portfolio annually or every few years, depending on market conditions and your retirement timeline.

The Role of Dividend-Paying Stocks

While reducing risk is important, you still need your portfolio to grow. One strategy is to include dividend-paying stocks in your portfolio. These stocks provide regular income through dividends, which can be reinvested or used to cover expenses in retirement.

Example: Sarah, a retiree, shifted 30% of her equity holdings into dividend-paying stocks as she neared retirement. These stocks provided a steady stream of income, which she used to cover her living expenses, reducing her need to sell shares during market downturns.

Application for You:

- **Identify Quality Dividend Stocks**: Look for companies with a history of paying and increasing dividends over time. These companies tend to be more stable and can provide a reliable income stream.
  - **Action Step**: Research dividend-focused mutual funds or exchange-traded funds (ETFs) if you prefer diversification without picking individual stocks. Discuss these options with your financial advisor to see how they might fit into your overall strategy.

2. Adapting to Market Changes

Markets are inherently unpredictable. While you can't control market movements, you can control how you respond to them. Adapting your retirement plan to changing market conditions is key to maintaining financial stability.

Staying Informed Without Overreacting

Example: John, a recent retiree, noticed a significant drop in the stock market and felt the urge to sell his investments to avoid further losses. However, his advisor reminded him of the long-term nature of his investment strategy and the dangers of reacting to short-term market fluctuations. By staying the course, John avoided locking in losses and benefited from the market's eventual recovery.

Application for You:

- **Monitor, But Don't Panic**: Keep an eye on market trends and your portfolio's performance, but resist the urge to make drastic changes based on short-term movements.
  - **Action Step**: Set a regular review schedule (e.g., quarterly or semi-annually) with your financial advisor to evaluate your portfolio. During these reviews, assess whether any changes are needed based on your long-term goals, not short-term market fluctuations.

Flexibility in Your Withdrawal Strategy

One of the most critical aspects of retirement planning is deciding how and when to withdraw money from your retirement accounts. This decision can be influenced by market performance, tax considerations, and your spending needs.

Example: During a market downturn, Lisa, another retiree, decided to reduce her withdrawals from her investment accounts. Instead, she relied more on cash reserves and Social Security to cover her expenses. This allowed her investment accounts time to recover before she resumed her regular withdrawal rate.

Application for You:

- **Use a Dynamic Withdrawal Strategy**: Instead of a fixed withdrawal amount, consider adjusting your withdrawals based on market conditions. For instance, in years when your portfolio performs well, you might withdraw a bit more, while in down years, you withdraw less to preserve your principal.

    ○ **Action Step**: Discuss with your advisor the possibility of using a percentage-based withdrawal strategy, where you withdraw a fixed percentage of your portfolio's value each year. This approach naturally adjusts your withdrawals based on market performance.

- **Build a Cash Reserve**: Having a cash reserve of one to two years' worth of living expenses can provide a cushion during market downturns, allowing you to avoid selling investments at a loss.

    ○ **Action Step**: Calculate your annual living expenses and determine how much cash you should set aside. This cash reserve can be kept in a high-yield savings account or short-term CDs.

3. Protecting Your Capital

As you approach or enter retirement, preserving your capital becomes increasingly important. Protecting your savings from significant losses ensures that you'll have enough to last throughout your retirement.

The Role of Bonds and Fixed-Income Investments

Bonds and other fixed-income investments provide stability to your portfolio. While they offer lower returns than stocks, they are also less volatile, making them a safer option for retirees.

Example: Jim and Karen, both in their late 60s, moved 40% of their portfolio into a mix of high-quality corporate bonds and government bonds. This allocation provided them with steady income and reduced the overall risk of their portfolio, giving them peace of mind during periods of stock market volatility.

Application for You:

- **Diversify Your Bond Holdings**: Consider a mix of government bonds, corporate bonds, and bond funds to spread risk and capture different yield opportunities.
    - **Action Step**: Review bond options with your advisor and consider laddering bonds—buying bonds with different maturity dates—to ensure you have access to funds at various points in the future.

Consideration of Annuities for Guaranteed Income

Annuities can provide a guaranteed income stream for life, which can be a valuable addition to your retirement plan, especially if you're concerned about outliving your savings.

Example: After retiring, Paul purchased a fixed annuity that provides him with a guaranteed monthly income for the rest of his life. This income, combined with Social Security, covers his essential living expenses, allowing him to invest the rest of his portfolio with more flexibility.

Application for You:

- **Evaluate Annuity Options**: Fixed annuities, variable annuities, and indexed annuities each offer different benefits and risks. It's important to understand these differences and choose the option that best fits your retirement needs.

      ◦ **Action Step**: If you're considering an annuity, work with a financial advisor to compare products, focusing on fees, payout options, and the insurance company's financial strength. Annuities are complex products, so professional guidance is essential.

Long-Term Care Planning

As you age, the likelihood of needing long-term care increases. The cost of long-term care can be substantial, and without proper planning, it can quickly deplete your savings.

Example: Linda and her husband purchased long-term care insurance in their late 50s. When Linda was diagnosed with Alzheimer's at age 72, the insurance policy covered a significant portion of her care costs, preserving their savings for other expenses and preventing financial strain on her husband.

Application for You:

- **Consider Long-Term Care Insurance**: If you're concerned about the potential costs of long-term care, purchasing a long-term care insurance policy can protect your savings. The earlier you purchase, the lower the premiums will likely be.
  - ◦ **Action Step**: Explore long-term care insurance options with your advisor. Compare the coverage, premiums, and the financial health of the insurance providers. Some policies also offer hybrid options, combining life insurance with long-term care coverage, which can provide additional flexibility.

Conclusion: Building a Flexible and Resilient Retirement Plan

Strategic retirement planning is about more than just saving money; it's about creating a plan that can adapt to changing circumstances and protect your financial future. By balancing growth with stability, staying flexible in your withdrawal strategy, and focusing on capital preservation, you can ensure that your retirement savings will last as long as you do.

- **Action Step**: Review your current retirement plan with these strategies in mind. Are you balancing growth and stability effectively? Is your withdrawal strategy flexible enough to adapt to market changes? Do you have measures in place to protect your capital?

Taking these steps will help you build a resilient retirement plan that can withstand market fluctuations and ensure a secure and fulfilling retirement. In the next chapter, we'll explore the complex world of taxes in retirement and how you can optimize your strategy to keep more of your hard-earned money.

CHAPTER 3

Taxes in Retirement

Taxes are an unavoidable part of life, and they don't stop when you retire. In fact, taxes can become even more complex in retirement as you begin to draw income from various sources like Social Security, pensions, and retirement accounts. However, with careful planning, you can minimize your tax burden and keep more of your hard-earned money.

In this chapter, we'll explore how taxes impact your retirement income, key strategies to manage your tax liabilities, and specific actions you can take to optimize your retirement plan.

1. Understanding Required Minimum Distributions (RMDs)

One of the most important tax considerations in retirement is understanding Required Minimum Distributions (RMDs). RMDs are the minimum amounts that you must withdraw annually from your traditional IRA, 401(k), and other qualified retirement plans once you reach a certain age.

What Are RMDs and Why They Matter?

RMDs are mandated by the IRS to ensure that individuals don't defer taxes indefinitely. The age at which you must start taking

RMDs has changed over time. As of the latest tax laws, RMDs must begin by April 1 of the year following the year you turn 73. Failing to take your RMDs can result in severe penalties, so it's crucial to stay on top of this requirement.

Example: Suppose you turned 73 in 2024. You would be required to take your first RMD by April 1, 2025. The amount of your RMD is calculated based on your account balance as of December 31 of the previous year and the IRS's life expectancy factor. If you have a traditional IRA with a balance of $500,000 and your life expectancy factor is 25.6, your RMD for that year would be approximately $19,531 ($500,000 ÷ 25.6).

Application for You:

- **Calculate Your RMDs**: To avoid penalties, calculate your RMDs well in advance and set reminders to withdraw the required amount each year.
    - ◦ **Action Step**: Use the IRS's online RMD worksheet or consult with your financial advisor to calculate your RMDs. Make sure you understand the timeline for each account you hold.
- **Plan for the Tax Impact**: Withdrawals from traditional retirement accounts are taxed as ordinary income, which can push you into a higher tax bracket.
    - ◦ **Example**: If your RMD increases your taxable income, it might result in higher Medicare premiums or a larger tax bill. To mitigate this, consider spreading your withdrawals throughout the year or taking advantage of tax-deferred accounts like Roth IRAs.
    - ◦ **Action Step**: Develop a withdrawal strategy that considers the tax implications of your RMDs. You might choose to withdraw more in years when your tax rate

is lower or spread your withdrawals across multiple accounts to manage your taxable income.

2. Roth Conversions: A Smart Tax Strategy

Roth conversions can be an effective strategy to reduce your tax burden in retirement. By converting a portion of your traditional IRA or 401(k) to a Roth IRA, you pay taxes on the converted amount now, but your future withdrawals from the Roth IRA are tax-free.

What Is a Roth Conversion?

A Roth conversion involves moving funds from a traditional retirement account (like a traditional IRA or 401(k)) to a Roth IRA. The amount converted is treated as taxable income in the year of the conversion, but once the money is in the Roth IRA, it grows tax-free, and withdrawals in retirement are also tax-free, provided certain conditions are met.

Example: Let's say you retire at age 62 and have a traditional IRA with $500,000. You anticipate being in a lower tax bracket during the early years of retirement before RMDs begin at age 73. You decide to convert $50,000 from your traditional IRA to a Roth IRA each year for the next five years. You'll pay taxes on the $50,000 each year at your current tax rate, but future withdrawals from the Roth IRA will be tax-free.

Application for You:

- **Assess Your Tax Bracket**: Consider converting to a Roth IRA in years when your taxable income is lower, such as early retirement years before Social Security and RMDs begin.

- ◦ **Action Step**: Calculate your projected income for the next several years and identify periods when you expect to be in a lower tax bracket. Work with a tax advisor to determine the optimal amount to convert each year without pushing yourself into a higher tax bracket.
- **Use Partial Conversions**: Instead of converting your entire IRA at once, consider partial conversions spread over several years. This can help manage the tax impact and take advantage of lower tax brackets.
  - ◦ **Action Step**: Develop a multi-year conversion strategy, converting smaller amounts annually to avoid large tax bills. Adjust this plan as your income and tax situation evolve.
- **Evaluate the Benefits**: Converting to a Roth IRA can be particularly beneficial if you expect your tax rate to increase in the future or if you want to leave tax-free income to your heirs.
  - ◦ **Action Step**: If legacy planning is important to you, a Roth conversion can ensure that your beneficiaries receive tax-free income. Discuss this with your financial planner to weigh the benefits and costs.

3. Tax-Efficient Withdrawal Strategies

In retirement, the order in which you withdraw money from different accounts can have a significant impact on your overall tax liability. By carefully planning your withdrawals, you can minimize taxes and make your savings last longer.

The Order of Withdrawals

When you retire, you'll likely have several sources of income: Social Security, pensions, taxable investment accounts, and tax-deferred retirement accounts. The sequence in which you withdraw from these accounts matters.

Example: Consider a retiree named Anne, who has $300,000 in a taxable brokerage account, $400,000 in a traditional IRA, and $200,000 in a Roth IRA. By strategically withdrawing from her taxable account first, she allows her traditional IRA to continue growing tax-deferred and her Roth IRA to grow tax-free.

- **Step 1: Withdraw from Taxable Accounts First**: Start by withdrawing from your taxable accounts (like brokerage accounts). This allows your tax-deferred and tax-free accounts to continue growing.
- **Step 2: Use Tax-Deferred Accounts Next**: Once your taxable accounts are depleted or when RMDs begin, start withdrawing from tax-deferred accounts like traditional IRAs or 401(k)s. Remember that withdrawals from these accounts are subject to ordinary income tax.
- **Step 3: Tap Into Roth Accounts Last**: Save Roth IRAs for last, as they grow tax-free and do not have RMDs. This allows you to maximize the tax-free growth of these assets.

Application for You:

- **Create a Withdrawal Plan**: Map out your retirement income sources and determine the most tax-efficient order to withdraw from them. This plan should be revisited annually to adjust for changes in your financial situation or tax laws.
  - **Action Step**: Use a financial planning tool or consult with your advisor to create a detailed withdrawal strategy. Review this plan annually to ensure it remains op-

timal given current tax laws and your personal situation.

- **Consider Tax-Loss Harvesting**: If you have taxable investments, consider selling investments at a loss to offset gains and reduce your taxable income.
  - ○ **Action Step**: Review your taxable accounts for opportunities to sell investments that have declined in value. Use the losses to offset gains from other investments or to reduce your ordinary income up to $3,000 per year.

4. The Impact of Social Security on Taxes

Social Security benefits are a crucial part of most retirement plans, but they can also be subject to taxes depending on your overall income. Understanding how Social Security is taxed can help you plan your withdrawals and manage your taxable income more effectively.

How Social Security Benefits Are Taxed

The taxation of Social Security benefits depends on your combined income, which is calculated by adding half of your Social Security benefits to your other income, including tax-exempt interest. Depending on your combined income and filing status, up to 85% of your Social Security benefits may be taxable.

Example: Jack and Diane are married and file jointly. They have a combined income of $60,000, which includes $30,000 in Social Security benefits and $45,000 from other sources. Since their combined income is above the threshold, 85% of their Social Security benefits will be taxable.

Application for You:

- **Manage Your Combined Income**: To minimize the taxation of your Social Security benefits, manage your other sources of income carefully. For example, withdrawing from a Roth IRA won't increase your combined income because Roth withdrawals are tax-free.
  - ○ **Action Step**: Work with your advisor to estimate your combined income each year. Adjust your withdrawals from taxable accounts, tax-deferred accounts, and Roth IRAs to keep your combined income below key thresholds.
- **Consider Delaying Social Security**: Delaying Social Security benefits until age 70 can increase your monthly benefit and potentially reduce your taxable income in the early years of retirement.
  - ○ **Action Step**: Evaluate the benefits of delaying Social Security based on your life expectancy, income needs, and tax situation. Use online calculators or consult with your advisor to determine the optimal age to start benefits.

Conclusion: Creating a Tax-Efficient Retirement Plan

Taxes can significantly impact your retirement income, but with careful planning, you can minimize your tax burden and keep more of your money. By understanding RMDs, considering Roth conversions, developing a tax-efficient withdrawal strategy, and managing the taxation of Social Security, you can create a retirement plan that maximizes your after-tax income.

- **Action Step**: Review your current retirement accounts, Social Security benefits, and overall tax situation. Work with a financial advisor or tax professional to develop a personalized tax strategy that aligns with your retirement goals.

As you move forward in this book, we'll explore the critical role of insurance in retirement planning. From protecting your income to covering potential long-term care costs, the next chapter will help you understand how to use insurance to safeguard your financial future.

CHAPTER 4

Insurance Planning in Retirement

Insurance is a crucial component of any comprehensive retirement plan. As you transition from earning a steady income to living off your savings, the risks you face change. Ensuring that you and your loved ones are financially protected against unforeseen events is essential for maintaining peace of mind and financial stability throughout your retirement years.

In this chapter, we'll explore the various types of insurance that play a key role in retirement planning. We'll discuss how each type of insurance works, when and why you might need it, and how to choose the right coverage for your situation.

1. The Role of Insurance in Retirement

Insurance is not just about protecting your income during your working years; it's also about safeguarding your assets, ensuring that your healthcare needs are met, and providing for your loved ones in the event of your death. In retirement, insurance serves several key purposes:

- **Income Replacement**: Even in retirement, insurance can replace lost income for your spouse or dependents if something happens to you.
- **Healthcare Costs**: As you age, healthcare needs typically increase, making insurance critical for covering medical expenses.
- **Long-Term Care**: The cost of long-term care can quickly deplete your savings, but insurance can help cover these expenses.
- **Legacy Planning**: Life insurance can be used to pass wealth to your heirs or cover estate taxes, ensuring that your legacy is protected.

2. Term Life Insurance: Cost-Effective Coverage

Term life insurance provides coverage for a specific period, such as 10, 20, or 30 years. It is generally more affordable than permanent life insurance and pays a death benefit to your beneficiaries if you pass away during the term.

When to Consider Term Life Insurance

Term life insurance is ideal for covering specific financial obligations that may exist for a limited time, such as paying off a mortgage or ensuring your spouse has enough income if you pass away before retirement.

Example: Mike, a 58-year-old nearing retirement, has 10 years left on his mortgage. He purchases a 10-year term life insurance policy to cover the remaining mortgage balance. If something happens to him before the mortgage is paid off, his wife, Linda, won't have to worry about making mortgage payments out of their retirement savings.

Application for You:

- **Assess Your Needs**: Determine if you have specific financial obligations, such as a mortgage or dependent care, that would need to be covered if you passed away. If so, a term life policy could provide the coverage you need at a lower cost than permanent insurance.
  - ◦ **Action Step**: Calculate how much coverage you need by totaling your outstanding financial obligations. Then, compare term life insurance policies to find one that offers adequate coverage at an affordable price.
- **Consider Your Spouse's Financial Situation**: If your spouse would struggle financially without your income, a term life insurance policy could provide the necessary support during the remaining years of these obligations.
  - ◦ **Action Step**: Discuss with your spouse how much income they would need to maintain their standard of living if you were no longer there. Use this information to determine the appropriate policy amount and term length.

3. Whole Life Insurance: Permanent Protection and Cash Value

Whole life insurance is a type of permanent life insurance that provides lifelong coverage and includes a cash value component. Unlike term life insurance, whole life insurance doesn't expire as long as premiums are paid, and the cash value grows over time, allowing you to borrow against it if needed.

When to Consider Whole Life Insurance

Whole life insurance can be beneficial if you want to provide a guaranteed death benefit for your heirs, accumulate cash value, or have a permanent need for insurance, such as covering estate taxes or leaving a legacy.

Example: Susan, a 65-year-old retiree, wants to ensure her two children receive a financial inheritance and that her estate can cover any taxes or final expenses without burdening her heirs. She purchases a whole life insurance policy with a $500,000 death benefit. Over the years, the policy's cash value grows, providing her with a source of funds if she ever needs it.

Application for You:

- **Evaluate Long-Term Financial Goals**: Consider whether you have a permanent need for life insurance, such as leaving a legacy or ensuring your estate can cover taxes and final expenses. Whole life insurance can provide this coverage while also building cash value.
  - **Action Step**: Meet with a financial advisor to discuss your long-term financial goals and whether whole life insurance aligns with those goals. Consider how the cash value component might benefit you in retirement, offering a potential source of emergency funds.
- **Compare Costs**: Whole life insurance is more expensive than term life insurance. Be sure that the benefits, such as lifelong coverage and cash value growth, justify the higher premiums.
  - **Action Step**: Obtain quotes for both term and whole life insurance policies. Compare the premiums and benefits to determine which type of coverage best meets your needs and fits within your budget.

4. *Term Life with Living Benefits: Additional Protection*

Term life insurance with living benefits offers the same coverage as traditional term life insurance, but with added features that allow you to access a portion of the death benefit while you're still alive, under certain conditions. These conditions typically include being diagnosed with a terminal, chronic, or critical illness.

When to Consider Term Life with Living Benefits

This type of insurance can be particularly valuable if you're concerned about the financial impact of a serious illness during retirement. The living benefits can help cover medical costs or other expenses if you're unable to work or need specialized care.

Example: Jim, a 60-year-old retiree, purchases a 20-year term life insurance policy with living benefits. At age 68, he is diagnosed with a chronic illness that requires extensive treatment. Jim is able to access a portion of his policy's death benefit to help cover his medical expenses, reducing the financial burden on his wife, Carol.

Application for You:

- **Evaluate Your Health Risks**: If you're concerned about the possibility of a serious illness during retirement, a term life policy with living benefits could provide peace of mind and financial security.
  - ◦ **Action Step**: Consider your family's medical history and your current health status. Discuss with your financial advisor whether a term life policy with living benefits would be a good fit for your retirement plan.
- **Understand the Costs and Benefits**: Living benefits can provide valuable financial support, but they may come at a

higher premium or reduce the overall death benefit available to your heirs.

- ○ **Action Step**: Review the terms of policies that offer living benefits, including any additional costs or reductions in the death benefit. Compare these options with traditional term life insurance to determine if the added protection is worth the cost.

5. Disability Insurance: Protecting Your Income Before Retirement

Disability insurance provides income replacement if you become unable to work due to illness or injury. While most people associate disability insurance with their working years, it's worth considering even as you approach retirement, especially if you're planning to work part-time or delay full retirement.

When to Consider Disability Insurance

If you're still working or plan to continue working part-time in retirement, disability insurance can protect your income and ensure that you don't have to dip into your retirement savings if you're unable to work.

Example: Laura, a 62-year-old nearing retirement, plans to continue working part-time for a few more years to boost her retirement savings. She purchases a disability insurance policy that will provide 60% of her income if she becomes unable to work. At age 64, Laura suffers a back injury that forces her to stop working. Her disability insurance helps cover her living expenses while she recovers, allowing her to delay tapping into her retirement accounts.

Application for You:

- **Assess Your Continued Income Needs**: If you plan to work during retirement or are delaying full retirement, disability insurance can protect your income and help you avoid withdrawing from your retirement savings prematurely.
  - ◦ **Action Step**: Evaluate how much of your current or planned income you would need to replace if you were unable to work. Research disability insurance options that provide sufficient coverage to meet your needs.
- **Consider Short-Term vs. Long-Term Disability Insurance**: Short-term disability insurance typically covers a portion of your income for a few months, while long-term disability insurance can provide coverage for several years or until retirement age.
  - ◦ **Action Step**: Determine whether short-term, long-term, or a combination of both types of disability insurance is appropriate for your situation. Compare the costs and benefits of each option to find the best coverage.

6. Long-Term Care Insurance: Planning for Extended Care Needs

As you age, the likelihood of needing long-term care increases. Long-term care insurance helps cover the cost of services that assist with daily living activities, such as bathing, dressing, and eating, either at home or in a care facility.

When to Consider Long-Term Care Insurance

Long-term care can be expensive, and without insurance, these costs could quickly deplete your retirement savings. If you're concerned about the potential financial impact of needing long-term care, purchasing long-term care insurance can provide peace of mind.

Example: Helen and Robert, both in their early 60s, purchase long-term care insurance policies to protect their retirement savings. At age 75, Robert suffers a stroke and requires long-term care. The insurance policy covers the cost of his care, allowing Helen to maintain their standard of living and preserving their savings for other expenses.

Application for You:

- **Consider Your Family History and Health**: If you have a family history of chronic illness or long-term care needs, or if you're concerned about the potential cost of care, long-term care insurance may be a wise investment.
  - ◦ **Action Step**: Review your family's medical history and consider your health outlook. Discuss with your financial advisor whether long-term care insurance is a good fit for your retirement plan.
- **Purchase Early for Lower Premiums**: The cost of long-term care insurance increases with age, so purchasing a policy earlier can result in lower premiums.
  - ◦ **Action Step**: If you're in your 50s or early 60s, get quotes for long-term care insurance now to lock in lower premiums. Compare policies from different insurers to find the best coverage for your needs.
- **Explore Hybrid Policies**: Some life insurance policies offer long-term care riders, combining death benefits with long-term care coverage. This can be a cost-effective way to cover both needs.
  - ◦ **Action Step**: Research hybrid insurance policies that combine life insurance with long-term care benefits.

Compare these options to standalone long-term care insurance, and determine which best meets your needs.

Selecting the right insurance products is critical for safeguarding your financial future, but with so many options available, it can be overwhelming to know where to start. That's why we recommend scheduling a **Retirement Mastery Consultation**. Our experts will help you navigate the complexities of insurance planning and ensure that your coverage aligns with your overall retirement strategy.

Conclusion: Integrating Insurance Into Your Retirement Plan

Insurance is a crucial tool for protecting your retirement savings and ensuring that you and your loved ones are financially secure. By understanding the different types of insurance available—whether it's term life, whole life, term with living benefits, disability, or long-term care—you can make informed decisions about the coverage you need in retirement.

- **Action Step:** Take time to review your current insurance policies and assess whether they align with your retirement goals. Identify any gaps in coverage and explore options to fill those gaps, whether through new policies or adjustments to existing ones.

As you move forward in this book, we'll delve into the key ages and milestones that are critical in retirement planning. From when to claim Social Security to managing RMDs, the next chapter will help you navigate these important decisions and ensure that your retirement plan stays on track.

CHAPTER 5

Key Ages and Milestones in Retirement

Retirement planning isn't just about saving money; it's also about making critical decisions at the right time. Certain ages and milestones carry significant implications for your retirement income, healthcare, and overall financial strategy. Understanding these key points will help you make informed choices that align with your goals and maximize your financial security.

In this chapter, we'll explore the most important ages and milestones in retirement planning, explain why they matter, and provide you with actionable steps to ensure you're prepared for each one.

1. Age 59½: Penalty-Free Withdrawals from Retirement Accounts

One of the first critical ages in retirement planning is 59½. This is the age at which you can begin taking withdrawals from your tax-deferred retirement accounts, such as traditional IRAs and 401(k)s, without incurring a 10% early withdrawal penalty. However, while you can avoid the penalty, you will still owe income taxes on the withdrawals.

Why This Age Matters

Understanding the rules around age 59½ is crucial if you plan to retire early or need access to your retirement funds before full retirement age. If you need to tap into your retirement savings before this age, the penalties can significantly reduce your nest egg.

Example: Emily, age 58, is considering an early retirement but realizes that if she withdraws from her 401(k) before age 59½, she'll face a 10% penalty on top of regular income taxes. Instead, she decides to work for another 18 months, allowing her to access her 401(k) penalty-free once she turns 59½.

Application for You:

- **Plan Your Withdrawals**: If you anticipate needing your retirement funds before age 59½, consider other sources of income to bridge the gap, such as taxable investment accounts, savings, or part-time work.
  - **Action Step**: Review your retirement savings and income needs. If you're approaching age 59½ and considering withdrawals, consult with your financial advisor to plan the most tax-efficient strategy.
- **Explore the 72(t) Rule**: If you need to access your retirement funds before 59½ and can't avoid it, you might be able to use the 72(t) rule, which allows for a series of substantially equal periodic payments (SEPP) from your retirement account without penalty.
  - **Action Step**: Research the 72(t) rule and its requirements. Discuss with your advisor whether this strategy makes sense for your situation, considering the potential impact on your long-term retirement savings.

2. Age 62: Earliest Age to Claim Social Security

Age 62 marks the earliest age at which you can claim Social Security benefits. However, claiming early comes with a reduction in your monthly benefit—up to 30% less than if you wait until your full retirement age (FRA). Deciding when to claim Social Security is one of the most important decisions in retirement planning, as it affects your income for the rest of your life.

When to Claim Social Security

The decision to claim Social Security at age 62 depends on various factors, including your health, financial needs, and whether you plan to continue working. Claiming early can be beneficial if you need the income or have a shorter life expectancy, but waiting can result in higher lifetime benefits.

Example: David is 62 and considering claiming Social Security. He's in good health and plans to work until 67. After consulting with his financial advisor, David decides to delay claiming until his full retirement age of 67 to receive a higher monthly benefit. This decision will provide him with greater financial security throughout retirement.

Application for You:

- **Evaluate Your Health and Life Expectancy**: If you're in good health and have a family history of longevity, delaying Social Security could maximize your benefits. Conversely, if you have health concerns or need the income, claiming at 62 might be the better option.
  - **Action Step**: Use online Social Security calculators to estimate your benefits at different ages. Consider your

health, financial needs, and retirement goals when deciding the best time to claim.

- **Consider the Impact on Spousal Benefits**: If you're married, your decision to claim Social Security can affect your spouse's benefits, especially if they are entitled to spousal or survivor benefits.
  - ◦ **Action Step**: Discuss with your spouse how your Social Security decisions will impact their benefits. If you're the higher earner, delaying your benefits could increase the survivor benefits your spouse would receive if you pass away first.

3. Age 65: Medicare Eligibility

At age 65, you become eligible for Medicare, the federal health insurance program for seniors. Enrolling in Medicare on time is crucial to avoid late enrollment penalties, which can increase your premiums permanently. Medicare consists of several parts, including Part A (hospital insurance), Part B (medical insurance), and Part D (prescription drug coverage).

Medicare Enrollment Periods

Your Initial Enrollment Period (IEP) for Medicare begins three months before you turn 65 and lasts for seven months. Missing this enrollment window can result in higher premiums and a gap in coverage.

Example: Jane turns 65 in October and plans to retire soon after. She knows her IEP starts in July, so she enrolls in Medicare Part A and Part B in August to ensure her coverage begins when she turns 65. By enrolling on time, Jane avoids late enrollment penalties and ensures she has health coverage as soon as she needs it.

Application for You:

- **Mark Your Calendar**: Keep track of your Medicare Initial Enrollment Period to ensure you enroll on time and avoid penalties.
  - ○ **Action Step**: Set a reminder to begin the Medicare enrollment process three months before your 65th birthday. Research the different parts of Medicare to determine which coverage options best suit your needs.
- **Consider Supplemental Insurance**: Original Medicare doesn't cover all healthcare expenses, such as copayments, coinsurance, and deductibles. You may want to explore Medicare Supplement Insurance (Medigap) or Medicare Advantage plans to cover these additional costs.
  - ○ **Action Step**: Compare Medigap and Medicare Advantage plans to find one that provides the coverage you need. Consider factors like cost, network restrictions, and additional benefits when making your decision.

4. Age 67: Full Retirement Age (FRA) for Social Security

For most people retiring today, full retirement age (FRA) for Social Security is between 66 and 67, depending on your birth year. At FRA, you're eligible to receive 100% of your Social Security benefit. Claiming before FRA results in reduced benefits, while delaying beyond FRA increases your benefits until age 70.

Maximizing Your Social Security Benefits

Reaching your full retirement age allows you to claim your full Social Security benefit without any reduction. If you continue working past FRA, your benefits may increase due to additional earnings.

Example: Linda, who was born in 1958, has a full retirement age of 66 years and 8 months. She decides to continue working until 68, allowing her Social Security benefits to increase further while she continues to earn income. By delaying, Linda maximizes her Social Security benefits and increases her financial security in retirement.

Application for You:

- **Decide When to Claim**: If you can afford to wait until FRA or later, doing so will increase your monthly Social Security benefits. Consider whether delaying benefits aligns with your retirement goals and financial needs.
  - ◦ **Action Step**: Review your retirement budget and projected income needs. If you can cover your expenses without claiming Social Security early, consider waiting until FRA or later to maximize your benefits.
- **Understand Earnings Limits**: If you claim Social Security before FRA and continue to work, be aware that your benefits may be temporarily reduced if your earnings exceed certain limits.
  - ◦ **Action Step**: If you plan to work while claiming Social Security before FRA, monitor your earnings to ensure they don't exceed the Social Security earnings limit, which could result in reduced benefits.

5. Age 70½: Charitable Distributions from IRAs

At age 70½, you can begin making Qualified Charitable Distributions (QCDs) from your traditional IRA. A QCD allows you to donate up to $100,000 per year directly to a qualified charity without including the distribution in your taxable income. This strategy can be particularly beneficial for those who wish to support charitable causes while reducing their taxable income.

How QCDs Can Benefit You

QCDs can help reduce your taxable income, which may lower your overall tax bill, including potential reductions in the taxation of Social Security benefits and Medicare premiums.

Example: George, age 71, regularly donates to his favorite charity. Instead of writing a check, he makes a $10,000 QCD from his traditional IRA. This donation counts toward his RMD for the year, but it doesn't increase his taxable income, allowing George to reduce his overall tax liability while supporting a cause he cares about.

Application for You:

- **Incorporate QCDs into Your Giving Strategy**: If you're charitably inclined and subject to RMDs, consider using QCDs to meet your charitable goals while reducing your taxable income.
  - **Action Step**: Work with your financial advisor to identify the charities you wish to support through QCDs. Ensure that the charity is a qualified organization to receive QCDs, and coordinate with your IRA custodian to process the distribution.

6. Age 72: Required Minimum Distributions (RMDs) Begin

As discussed in Chapter 3, you must begin taking Required Minimum Distributions (RMDs) from your traditional IRA, 401(k), and other qualified retirement plans starting at age 72. RMDs are the minimum amounts you must withdraw annually, and they are subject to ordinary income tax.

Managing RMDs to Minimize Taxes

RMDs can significantly increase your taxable income, potentially pushing you into a higher tax bracket or affecting the taxation of your Social Security benefits.

Example: Patricia, age 72, has a traditional IRA with a balance of $600,000. Her RMD for the year is $21,897. Patricia's financial advisor suggests a strategy to minimize her tax liability, including using part of her RMD for a QCD and spreading the rest of the withdrawals throughout the year to avoid a large tax hit all at once.

Application for You:

- **Plan for RMDs**: Start planning for RMDs several years before they begin. Consider strategies to reduce the tax impact, such as Roth conversions, QCDs, or spreading withdrawals over the year.
  - **Action Step**: Calculate your expected RMDs and their impact on your taxable income. Discuss with your advisor how to integrate RMDs into your overall retirement income strategy while minimizing taxes.
- **Automate Your Withdrawals**: Many financial institutions allow you to automate your RMDs, ensuring you don't miss the deadline and incur penalties.
  - **Action Step**: Set up automated RMDs through your IRA custodian to ensure timely withdrawals. Consider setting up monthly or quarterly distributions to help with cash flow management.

Conclusion: Navigating the Key Milestones in Retirement
Understanding and planning for these key ages and milestones in retirement is essential for maximizing your financial security and

achieving your retirement goals. By making informed decisions about when to claim Social Security, enroll in Medicare, and take RMDs, you can create a retirement plan that supports your desired lifestyle.

- **Action Step**: Review your current retirement plan and ensure that you're prepared for these key milestones. If you're approaching one of these ages, meet with your financial advisor to discuss your options and make any necessary adjustments to your strategy.

As you continue your journey through this book, we'll next explore the importance of managing cash flow in retirement. Understanding how to create and maintain a reliable income stream is crucial for ensuring that your retirement savings last throughout your lifetime.

CHAPTER 6

Managing Cash Flow in Retirement

M anaging cash flow in retirement is one of the most critical aspects of ensuring your financial security. Unlike your working years, when income is steady and predictable, retirement often requires drawing from multiple sources to fund your lifestyle. The key to a successful retirement is making sure your income covers your expenses without depleting your savings too quickly.

In this chapter, we'll explore how to create a retirement budget, establish reliable income streams, and manage debt effectively. By understanding these elements, you can maintain a steady cash flow that supports your desired lifestyle throughout your retirement years.

1. Creating a Retirement Budget

A retirement budget is the foundation of your cash flow plan. It helps you understand your income and expenses, ensuring that you can cover your needs while preserving your savings. The first step in managing cash flow is to create a realistic budget that reflects your retirement goals and lifestyle.

Why a Budget Is Crucial in Retirement

In retirement, your income may come from several sources, including Social Security, pensions, savings, and investments. Unlike a regular paycheck, these income sources can vary, making it essential to carefully track your spending to ensure you don't outlive your savings.

Example: Let's consider Bob and Nancy, who have just retired. They have a combined monthly income of $5,000 from Social Security and Bob's pension. However, after reviewing their expenses, they realize they are spending $6,500 per month. Without a budget, they might quickly dip into their savings to cover the shortfall, risking depleting their nest egg too early. By creating a detailed budget, they can identify areas to cut back and find ways to balance their income and expenses.

Application for You:

- **Track Your Expenses**: Begin by tracking your current expenses for a few months to understand where your money is going. Include all categories, such as housing, utilities, groceries, healthcare, insurance, and entertainment.
    - ◦ **Action Step**: Use a budgeting tool or app to categorize and track your expenses. Review your spending to identify any unnecessary expenses that can be reduced or eliminated.
- **Differentiate Between Needs and Wants**: Separate your essential expenses (needs) from discretionary spending (wants). This will help you prioritize your spending and make adjustments if your income is lower than expected.
    - ◦ **Action Step**: Create two lists—one for essential expenses (e.g., mortgage, utilities, groceries) and one for

discretionary expenses (e.g., dining out, travel). If necessary, prioritize essential expenses and consider adjusting discretionary spending to balance your budget.

- **Plan for Inflation**: Remember that prices for goods and services will likely rise over time. Include an inflation factor in your budget to ensure your income keeps pace with rising costs.
  - ○ **Action Step**: Increase your projected expenses by 2-3% annually to account for inflation. This will help you adjust your budget and ensure you have enough income to maintain your lifestyle over time.

2. Establishing Reliable Income Streams

Once you have a budget in place, the next step is to establish reliable income streams that will fund your retirement. Ideally, your income will come from a mix of guaranteed sources, like Social Security and pensions, as well as variable sources, like investment withdrawals.

Diversifying Your Income Sources

Having multiple income streams in retirement helps reduce the risk of running out of money. It also allows you to be more flexible in how you manage your cash flow.

Example: Mary, a retiree, has several income sources: Social Security, a small pension, dividend income from her stock portfolio, and rental income from a property she owns. By diversifying her income streams, Mary is less reliant on any single source of income and can adjust her withdrawals based on market conditions.

Application for You:

1. **Maximize Social Security:** Social Security is a stable source of income, so consider strategies to maximize your benefits, such as delaying benefits until age 70 if possible.
   Action Step: Use the Social Security Administration's online calculators or consult with your financial advisor to determine the best time to claim benefits based on your specific situation.

2. **Consider Annuities:** An annuity can provide guaranteed income for life, which can complement other sources of retirement income and reduce the risk of outliving your savings.
   Action Step: Evaluate different types of annuities (e.g., fixed, variable, indexed) to see if one fits into your retirement income strategy. Discuss with your advisor the potential benefits and drawbacks of including an annuity in your plan.

3. **Leverage Investment Income:** Withdrawals from your investment accounts can supplement your guaranteed income. However, it's important to manage these withdrawals carefully to avoid depleting your savings too quickly.
   Action Step: Develop a withdrawal strategy that considers your portfolio's asset allocation, market conditions, and your income needs. For example, the 4% rule is a common guideline, suggesting you withdraw 4% of your portfolio in the first year of retirement and adjust for inflation in subsequent years.

Selecting the right mix of income sources is crucial for maintaining financial stability throughout retirement, but this can often be a complex and overwhelming process. To ensure your income strategy is well-balanced and aligned with your long-term goals, consider scheduling a **Retirement Mastery Consultation**. During this personalized session, our experts will work with you to develop a tailored income plan that maximizes your Social Security benefits, explores the potential of annuities, and optimizes your investment withdrawals.

3. Managing Debt in Retirement

Carrying debt into retirement can strain your cash flow, particularly if your income is lower than it was during your working years. Paying off debt before or early in retirement can free up more of your income for living expenses and reduce financial stress.

Prioritizing Debt Repayment

Not all debt is created equal. High-interest debt, like credit cards, should be prioritized for repayment, while lower-interest debt, like a mortgage, may be more manageable.

Example: John and Lisa are both retired, but they still have a mortgage and some credit card debt. They decide to use a portion of their retirement savings to pay off the credit card debt, which carries a high interest rate. They continue making monthly payments on their mortgage but choose not to pay it off early, as their mortgage interest rate is low and they receive a tax deduction on the interest.

Application for You:

- **Pay Off High-Interest Debt First**: Focus on paying off credit cards, personal loans, or any other debt with high interest rates as soon as possible. This will reduce the overall amount of interest you pay and free up more cash for other expenses.
  - **Action Step**: List all your debts, including interest rates and monthly payments. Develop a plan to pay off

high-interest debt first, potentially using a debt snow-
ball or debt avalanche method.

- **Consider Refinancing**: If you have a mortgage or other
loans with higher interest rates, consider refinancing to secure
a lower rate, which could reduce your monthly payments and
improve your cash flow.
  - ◦ **Action Step**: Contact your lender to explore refinanc-
    ing options. Compare the costs and benefits of refi-
    nancing, including any fees, to ensure it makes financial
    sense.
- **Avoid Taking on New Debt**: Be cautious about taking on
new debt in retirement, as it can strain your cash flow and reduce your financial flexibility.
  - ◦ **Action Step**: Before making large purchases, consider
    whether they are necessary and if there are alternative
    ways to pay for them, such as saving up or using cash in-
    stead of credit.

4. Building a Cash Reserve

A cash reserve is an essential component of your retirement plan.
It provides a financial cushion that you can draw from during emergencies or periods of market volatility, allowing you to avoid selling
investments at a loss.

How Much Should You Keep in Cash?

The amount of cash you should keep on hand depends on your
monthly expenses, risk tolerance, and other income sources. A common rule of thumb is to keep 6-12 months' worth of living expenses
in a cash reserve.

Example: Tom and Carol, both in their early 70s, keep $50,000 in a high-yield savings account as a cash reserve. This amount covers about 12 months of their living expenses. During a recent market downturn, they were able to use their cash reserve instead of selling investments at a loss, allowing their portfolio time to recover.

Application for You:

- **Determine Your Cash Reserve Needs**: Calculate how much you need to cover your essential expenses for 6-12 months. This reserve should be easily accessible, such as in a savings account or money market fund.
  - ◦ **Action Step**: Review your budget and monthly expenses to determine the appropriate size of your cash reserve. Set aside this amount in a safe, liquid account that offers easy access when needed.
- **Use Your Reserve Wisely**: Only tap into your cash reserve for emergencies or to avoid withdrawing from investments during a market downturn. Replenish the reserve as soon as possible after using it.
  - ◦ **Action Step**: Set guidelines for when you'll use your cash reserve, such as for medical emergencies or major unexpected expenses. Rebuild your reserve as part of your regular financial routine, just as you would with other savings goals.

5. Setting Up Systematic Withdrawals

Systematic withdrawals involve setting up regular, automatic withdrawals from your retirement accounts. This strategy helps ensure a steady income stream while maintaining discipline in managing your retirement savings.

Benefits of Systematic Withdrawals

Systematic withdrawals can help you manage your cash flow, reduce the risk of overspending, and make it easier to stick to your budget. By automating your withdrawals, you can create a predictable income stream that aligns with your budget and spending needs.

Example: Alice has a $600,000 retirement portfolio and plans to withdraw $24,000 annually (4% of her portfolio) to supplement her Social Security income. She sets up a systematic withdrawal plan, which automatically transfers $2,000 per month from her investment account to her checking account. This regular income helps her cover her monthly expenses without needing to make ad-hoc withdrawals.

Application for You:

- **Determine Your Withdrawal Rate**: Based on your retirement budget and portfolio size, determine a sustainable withdrawal rate that balances your income needs with the longevity of your savings.
  - **Action Step**: Consider the 4% rule as a starting point, but adjust based on your risk tolerance, market conditions, and personal circumstances. Work with your advisor to fine-tune your withdrawal rate.
- **Set Up Automatic Withdrawals**: Automating your withdrawals can help you stick to your budget and avoid the temptation to withdraw more than you need.
  - **Action Step**: Contact your financial institution to set up automatic withdrawals from your retirement accounts. Choose a withdrawal frequency (monthly,

quarterly, etc.) that aligns with your income needs and cash flow management.

Conclusion: Ensuring a Steady Cash Flow Throughout Retirement

Managing cash flow in retirement requires careful planning, discipline, and flexibility. By creating a detailed budget, establishing multiple income streams, managing debt, building a cash reserve, and setting up systematic withdrawals, you can ensure that your retirement savings last and support your desired lifestyle.

- **Action Step**: Review your current cash flow plan and make any necessary adjustments based on the strategies discussed in this chapter. Regularly revisit your plan to ensure it continues to meet your needs as you move through retirement.

As you continue with this book, the next chapter will explore smart investment options for retirement, including annuities, indexed accounts, and structured notes. Understanding these options will help you make informed decisions about how to grow and protect your retirement savings.

CHAPTER 7

Smart Investment
Options for Retirement

Investing during retirement is a delicate balance between generating enough income to support your lifestyle and preserving your capital to ensure your savings last. Unlike your working years, when you may have been more focused on growth, retirement requires a more cautious approach that prioritizes income, stability, and risk management.

In this chapter, we'll explore several smart investment options that can help you achieve these goals. We'll discuss the pros and cons of each, provide real-world examples, and offer actionable steps to help you incorporate these investments into your retirement strategy.

1. Annuities: Reliable Income for Your Golden Years

Annuities are insurance products designed to provide a steady income stream, often for life. They can be a valuable addition to your retirement portfolio, particularly if you're concerned about outliving your savings or want a guaranteed income to cover essential expenses.

Types of Annuities

There are several types of annuities, each with its own set of features, benefits, and risks. The most common types include:

- **Fixed Annuities**: These provide a guaranteed, fixed income for a specified period or for life. The payments do not fluctuate with market conditions.
- **Variable Annuities**: These allow you to invest in various sub-accounts, similar to mutual funds. Your income can vary based on the performance of these investments.
- **Indexed Annuities**: These offer returns based on the performance of a market index, like the S&P 500, but typically have a cap on potential gains and a floor to protect against losses.

Example: Tom, a retiree, is concerned about running out of money in his later years. He decides to invest a portion of his retirement savings into a fixed annuity that guarantees him $2,000 per month for the rest of his life. This income covers his basic living expenses, giving him peace of mind that he won't outlive his savings.

Application for You:

- **Evaluate Your Income Needs**: Determine how much of your retirement income should come from guaranteed sources like annuities. Consider your essential expenses and how much risk you're willing to take with the rest of your portfolio.
  - **Action Step**: Work with a financial advisor to assess your income needs and explore whether a fixed, variable, or indexed annuity fits into your retirement plan. Calculate how much of your savings should be allo-

cated to an annuity to provide the desired level of income.

- **Understand the Costs and Features**: Annuities can come with fees, including surrender charges, administrative fees, and mortality and expense risk charges. It's important to understand these costs and how they affect your returns.
  - ◦ **Action Step**: Before purchasing an annuity, request a detailed breakdown of all fees and charges. Compare the costs and benefits of different annuity products to ensure you're getting the best value for your money.
- **Consider Longevity Risk**: If you're concerned about living a long life and outliving your savings, an annuity can help mitigate this risk by providing a lifetime income stream.
  - ◦ **Action Step**: Evaluate your health and family history to determine if a lifetime income annuity makes sense for you. Discuss with your advisor how an annuity could fit into your overall retirement income strategy.

2. Indexed Accounts: Balancing Growth and Security

Indexed accounts, such as indexed annuities or indexed universal life insurance (IUL), offer a way to participate in market gains while providing some protection against market losses. These accounts credit interest based on the performance of a market index, such as the S&P 500, but typically include a cap on gains and a floor to prevent losses.

How Indexed Accounts Work

Indexed accounts are designed to offer a balance between growth potential and security. You won't experience the full upside of the market, but you're also protected from significant losses in down markets. This can be particularly appealing in retirement when preserving capital is a priority.

Example: Sarah, a 65-year-old retiree, wants to continue growing her savings but is wary of stock market volatility. She invests in an indexed annuity that offers a 5% cap on gains and a 0% floor. If the S&P 500 increases by 10%, she earns 5% for the year. If the market declines, her account value remains the same, with no losses.

Application for You:

- **Assess Your Risk Tolerance**: If you're looking for growth potential with some downside protection, indexed accounts might be a good fit. However, be aware of the caps on gains and how they affect your overall returns.
  - ◦ **Action Step**: Review your investment goals and risk tolerance with your advisor. Determine if indexed accounts align with your desire for growth and capital preservation in retirement.
- **Understand the Participation Rate and Cap**: Indexed accounts often come with a participation rate (the percentage of index gains credited to your account) and a cap on how much you can earn. It's important to understand these limits and how they impact your returns.
  - ◦ **Action Step**: Before investing in an indexed account, ask for a clear explanation of the participation rate and cap. Consider how these factors affect the potential growth of your investment and whether it meets your retirement goals.
- **Compare Indexed Accounts with Other Investments**: Indexed accounts are just one option for balancing growth and security. Compare them with other conservative investments,

such as bonds or dividend-paying stocks, to determine which option best suits your needs.

- ◦ **Action Step**: Conduct a side-by-side comparison of indexed accounts, bonds, and other fixed-income investments. Evaluate the potential returns, risks, and costs of each to determine the most suitable investment for your retirement portfolio.

3. Structured Notes: A Blend of Bonds and Derivatives

Structured notes are complex financial instruments that combine bonds with derivatives to offer customized investment solutions. They can provide exposure to various asset classes, such as stocks, commodities, or currencies, while offering some level of capital protection.

Understanding Structured Notes

Structured notes are typically issued by financial institutions and can be designed to meet specific investment goals, such as income generation, capital preservation, or market participation. They offer the potential for higher returns than traditional bonds, but they also come with higher risks and complexity.

Example: Robert, a retiree, is interested in an investment that offers both growth potential and some downside protection. He invests in a structured note tied to the performance of a basket of stocks. The note offers 50% downside protection, meaning that if the basket of stocks declines by up to 50%, he doesn't lose any capital. However, if the decline exceeds 50%, his losses are proportional to the drop beyond that point.

Application for You:

- **Consider Your Investment Objectives**: Structured notes can be tailored to specific investment goals, but they are complex products. Determine what you want to achieve—income, growth, or capital protection—before considering structured notes.
  - ○ **Action Step**: Discuss with your advisor whether structured notes align with your investment objectives. If you're considering structured notes, ensure you fully understand the terms, risks, and potential returns.
- **Understand the Risks**: Structured notes are not without risk. They are subject to the credit risk of the issuer, and in some cases, you could lose a significant portion of your investment if the underlying assets perform poorly.
  - ○ **Action Step**: Research the financial strength of the issuing institution and the specific terms of the structured note. Ensure you're comfortable with the level of risk before investing.
- **Compare with Other Investment Options**: Structured notes can offer attractive features, but they are not the only option for achieving your investment goals. Compare structured notes with other investments, such as bonds, mutual funds, or ETFs, to see if they offer better risk-adjusted returns.
  - ○ **Action Step**: Create a comparison chart that includes structured notes and other investment options you're considering. Evaluate the pros and cons of each, focusing on potential returns, risks, and how they fit into your overall retirement plan.

4. Dividend-Paying Stocks: Income with Growth Potential

Dividend-paying stocks offer the potential for capital appreciation along with regular income. These stocks are often issued by well-established companies with a history of paying consistent and growing dividends. For retirees, dividend-paying stocks can provide a steady income stream while also offering the potential for growth.

Why Dividends Matter in Retirement

Dividends can be a reliable source of income in retirement, especially when interest rates are low, and bond yields are not sufficient to meet your income needs. Additionally, dividend-paying stocks have the potential to increase in value over time, helping your portfolio keep pace with inflation.

Example: Helen, a retiree, invests in a portfolio of blue-chip stocks that pay an average dividend yield of 4%. These dividends provide her with $12,000 annually, which she uses to cover part of her living expenses. Over time, as the companies increase their dividends, Helen's income grows, helping her maintain her purchasing power in retirement.

Application for You:

- **Focus on Quality Companies**: Invest in companies with a strong history of paying and increasing dividends. Look for firms with stable earnings, strong cash flow, and a commitment to returning capital to shareholders.
  - **Action Step**: Research dividend-paying stocks or consider dividend-focused mutual funds or ETFs. Evaluate each company's dividend history, payout ratio, and financial health before investing.
- **Reinvest Dividends if Possible**: If you don't need the income immediately, consider reinvesting dividends to buy more shares. This strategy can help grow your investment over time, compounding your returns.

- ◦ **Action Step**: Set up a dividend reinvestment plan (DRIP) with your brokerage to automatically reinvest dividends into additional shares of the same stock. Review your reinvestment strategy annually to ensure it aligns with your income needs.
- **Diversify Your Dividend Portfolio**: Don't rely on just a few dividend-paying stocks. Diversify across sectors and industries to reduce risk and ensure a steady income stream.
  - ◦ **Action Step**: Build a diversified portfolio of dividend-paying stocks across different industries, such as utilities, consumer staples, and healthcare. Consider using a dividend-focused ETF to achieve instant diversification.

5. Bonds and Bond Funds: Stability and Income

Bonds are a cornerstone of a retirement portfolio because they offer a stable income stream and lower risk compared to stocks. When you buy a bond, you're lending money to an issuer (such as a government or corporation) in exchange for regular interest payments and the return of principal at maturity.

Types of Bonds and Their Role in Retirement

There are several types of bonds to consider, including:

- **Government Bonds**: Issued by the federal government and considered low-risk. Examples include U.S. Treasury bonds.
- **Municipal Bonds**: Issued by state and local governments. They often offer tax-free interest income.

- **Corporate Bonds**: Issued by companies to raise capital. They offer higher yields than government bonds but come with higher risk.

Example: James, a retiree, allocates 40% of his portfolio to a mix of government and corporate bonds. This allocation provides him with a stable income stream through interest payments while preserving his capital. James also invests in a bond fund to diversify his holdings and reduce the risk associated with any single bond issuer.

Application for You:

- **Choose the Right Mix of Bonds**: Depending on your risk tolerance and income needs, decide on the right mix of government, municipal, and corporate bonds for your portfolio.
  - ○ **Action Step**: Work with your financial advisor to determine the appropriate bond allocation based on your retirement goals, time horizon, and risk tolerance. Consider laddering bonds (buying bonds with different maturities) to manage interest rate risk and provide a steady income stream.
- **Consider Bond Funds or ETFs**: Bond funds and ETFs offer diversification across many issuers and maturities, which can reduce risk and simplify management.
  - ○ **Action Step**: Research bond funds or ETFs that align with your investment objectives. Look at factors such as yield, duration, credit quality, and fees before making a decision.
- **Monitor Interest Rate Changes**: Bond prices and yields are influenced by interest rates. When rates rise, bond prices typically fall, and vice versa. Understanding this relationship can help you manage your bond investments.

- **Action Step**: Stay informed about interest rate trends and consider how they may impact your bond investments. If you're concerned about rising rates, consider shorter-duration bonds or bond funds to reduce interest rate risk.

Conclusion: Building a Balanced Retirement Portfolio

Selecting the right mix of investment options in retirement is key to balancing income, growth, and risk. By understanding and incorporating various investment vehicles—such as annuities, indexed accounts, structured notes, dividend-paying stocks, and bonds—you can create a diversified portfolio that supports your financial goals and provides the stability you need in retirement.

- **Action Step**: Review your current retirement portfolio and assess whether it aligns with your income needs, risk tolerance, and long-term goals. Work with your financial advisor to make any necessary adjustments, ensuring that your investment strategy is well-balanced and capable of supporting your retirement lifestyle.

As you move forward in this book, the final chapter will explore how to craft your financial legacy. We'll discuss estate planning, charitable giving, and strategies for passing on your wealth to the next generation, ensuring that your legacy is secure and meaningful.

CHAPTER 8

Crafting Your Financial Legacy

Planning for your financial legacy is about more than just transferring assets to your heirs; it's about ensuring that your wealth reflects your values and supports your loved ones and the causes you care about. A well-crafted legacy plan can provide peace of mind, knowing that your financial affairs will be handled according to your wishes, and your impact will be felt for generations.

In this chapter, we'll guide you through the key components of estate planning, from creating a will to setting up trusts, and from reducing estate taxes to making charitable donations. We'll provide practical examples and actionable steps to help you craft a financial legacy that aligns with your goals and values.

1. Estate Planning Essentials

Estate planning is the process of organizing your financial affairs so that your assets are distributed according to your wishes after your death. A comprehensive estate plan includes a will, possibly one or more trusts, beneficiary designations, and other legal documents that ensure your wishes are carried out.

Creating a Will

A will is a legal document that outlines how your assets will be distributed after your death. It's the cornerstone of any estate plan and ensures that your property is transferred according to your wishes, rather than according to state law.

Example: John, a retiree, creates a will that specifies how his assets will be distributed among his three children. He also names a guardian for his minor granddaughter, ensuring that she will be cared for by someone he trusts. By having a will in place, John ensures that his assets are distributed according to his wishes and that there is no confusion or conflict among his heirs.

Application for You:

- **Draft Your Will**: If you don't have a will, it's important to create one as soon as possible. If you already have a will, review it regularly to ensure it reflects your current wishes and circumstances.
    - ○ **Action Step**: Consult with an estate planning attorney to draft a will that accurately reflects your wishes. Be sure to include provisions for the care of any dependents, as well as instructions for the distribution of your assets.
- **Choose an Executor**: The executor of your will is responsible for carrying out your wishes, including distributing your assets and settling your debts. Choose someone you trust and who is capable of handling these responsibilities.
    - ○ **Action Step**: Select an executor and discuss your wishes with them. Ensure they are willing and able to take on this role, and include their name in your will.

Setting Up Trusts

Trusts are legal arrangements that allow you to transfer assets to a trustee, who manages them on behalf of your beneficiaries. Trusts can be used to reduce estate taxes, avoid probate, and protect your assets from creditors.

Example: Sarah and Tom, a retired couple, set up a revocable living trust to manage their assets during their lifetime and transfer them to their children after their death. By doing so, they avoid probate, ensuring a smoother and quicker transfer of assets. They also establish a special needs trust for their son, who has a disability, ensuring that his inheritance will not disqualify him from receiving government benefits.

Application for You:

- **Determine If a Trust Is Right for You**: Trusts can be useful in a variety of situations, such as if you have a large estate, want to avoid probate, or need to provide for a dependent with special needs.
    - **Action Step**: Discuss with your estate planning attorney whether a trust is appropriate for your situation. If so, determine which type of trust (e.g., revocable living trust, irrevocable trust, special needs trust) best meets your needs.
- **Fund Your Trust**: Once your trust is established, you need to transfer ownership of your assets to the trust. This process is known as funding the trust and is essential for ensuring that your assets are managed according to your wishes.
    - **Action Step**: Work with your attorney to transfer titles, deeds, and other assets into your trust. Regularly

review your trust to ensure it is fully funded and up to date.

2. Reducing Estate Taxes and Probate Costs

Without proper planning, a significant portion of your estate could be lost to taxes and probate costs. There are several strategies you can use to minimize these expenses and ensure more of your wealth is passed on to your heirs.

Understanding Estate Taxes

Federal estate taxes apply to estates that exceed a certain value threshold, which is adjusted annually. Some states also impose their own estate or inheritance taxes. Reducing the taxable value of your estate can help minimize or eliminate these taxes.

Example: George, who has a substantial estate, works with his financial advisor to gift $15,000 per year to each of his three grandchildren, reducing the value of his estate while providing financial support to his family. By making annual gifts and setting up a trust, George reduces his estate below the federal estate tax exemption limit, avoiding significant taxes after his death.

Application for You:

- **Understand the Estate Tax Exemption**: The federal estate tax exemption is currently quite high, but it can change over time. Understand the current exemption level and how it applies to your estate.
  - **Action Step**: Review your estate's value with your financial advisor. If your estate exceeds the exemption limit, discuss strategies for reducing its taxable value,

such as gifting, setting up trusts, or charitable donations.

- **Use Gifting to Reduce Your Estate**: The IRS allows you to gift up to a certain amount per year, per recipient, without incurring gift taxes. By making annual gifts, you can reduce the value of your estate while helping your loved ones.
  - ◦ **Action Step**: Consider making annual gifts to your heirs or loved ones. Consult with your advisor to understand the current gift tax limits and how gifting can be used as part of your estate planning strategy.
- **Plan for State Estate Taxes**: Some states have their own estate or inheritance taxes, which may have lower exemption limits than the federal estate tax.
  - ◦ **Action Step**: Research the estate tax laws in your state. If your state imposes estate taxes, consider strategies to reduce the impact, such as moving to a state without estate taxes or using trusts to shield assets.

Avoiding Probate

Probate is the legal process of distributing your assets after your death. It can be time-consuming, costly, and public. Fortunately, there are ways to avoid probate and ensure that your assets are transferred quickly and privately.

Example: Rebecca, a retiree, adds payable-on-death (POD) designations to her bank accounts and transfers ownership of her home to her revocable living trust. By doing so, she ensures that her assets can be transferred to her beneficiaries without going through probate, saving time and reducing costs.

Application for You:

- **Use Beneficiary Designations**: Assets like retirement accounts, life insurance policies, and bank accounts can often be transferred directly to your beneficiaries through beneficiary designations, bypassing probate.
  - **Action Step**: Review and update the beneficiary designations on all your accounts and policies. Ensure they reflect your current wishes and include contingencies in case your primary beneficiary predeceases you.
- **Consider Joint Ownership**: Jointly owned assets, such as a home or bank account, typically pass directly to the surviving owner without going through probate.
  - **Action Step**: If appropriate, consider adding joint ownership to certain assets. Be sure to understand the legal and tax implications of joint ownership before making changes.
- **Set Up a Living Trust**: A revocable living trust allows you to manage your assets during your lifetime and transfer them to your beneficiaries after your death without going through probate.
  - **Action Step**: Work with your estate planning attorney to establish and fund a living trust. Ensure that all relevant assets are transferred to the trust to avoid probate.

3. Charitable Giving: Leaving a Lasting Impact

Charitable giving is a powerful way to create a legacy that reflects your values and supports the causes you care about. With proper planning, charitable donations can also reduce your estate tax liability and provide financial benefits during your lifetime.

Types of Charitable Giving

There are several ways to structure your charitable giving, including direct donations, charitable trusts, and donor-advised funds.

Example: Bill and Susan, retirees with a passion for education, set up a charitable remainder trust (CRT) that provides them with income during their lifetime. Upon their death, the remaining assets in the trust will be donated to their favorite university. By setting up the CRT, they receive an immediate tax deduction, reduce their estate's taxable value, and leave a lasting legacy in the form of scholarships for future students.

Application for You:

- **Consider Direct Donations**: Making direct donations to charities during your lifetime can provide immediate tax benefits and allow you to see the impact of your generosity.
  - **Action Step**: Identify charities that align with your values and consider making direct donations. Keep records of your donations to claim tax deductions.
- **Explore Charitable Trusts**: Charitable remainder trusts (CRTs) and charitable lead trusts (CLTs) allow you to support a charity while providing income for yourself or your heirs.
  - **Action Step**: Discuss with your financial advisor and estate planning attorney whether a charitable trust is right for you. If so, work with them to establish the trust and designate your beneficiaries.
- **Set Up a Donor-Advised Fund**: A donor-advised fund (DAF) allows you to make a charitable contribution, receive an immediate tax deduction, and recommend grants to charities over time.

○ **Action Step**: Research donor-advised funds and consider opening one if you want to manage your charitable giving over time. This can be a flexible and tax-efficient way to support multiple causes.

4. Ensuring Your Wishes Are Honored

Even with a comprehensive estate plan in place, it's important to ensure that your wishes are clearly communicated and understood by your loved ones. This can help prevent misunderstandings, conflicts, and legal challenges after your death.

Communicating with Your Family

Having open conversations with your family about your estate plan can help set expectations and reduce the potential for disputes.

Example: Margaret, a widow with three children, schedules a family meeting to discuss her estate plan. She explains her decisions regarding the distribution of her assets and answers any questions her children have. By being transparent and involving her family in the planning process, Margaret reduces the likelihood of conflicts and ensures that her wishes are understood and respected.

Application for You:

• **Schedule a Family Meeting**: Consider holding a family meeting to discuss your estate plan. This is an opportunity to explain your decisions, answer questions, and address any concerns.

　○ **Action Step**: Plan a meeting with your family members to discuss your estate plan. Be clear about your wishes and explain the reasoning behind your decisions.

Encourage open communication and make sure everyone understands their roles.

- **Write a Letter of Instruction**: A letter of instruction is an informal document that provides guidance to your executor and family. It can include details like the location of important documents, funeral wishes, and other personal instructions.
  - ◦ **Action Step**: Write a letter of instruction to accompany your will. Include information about your assets, passwords, and any other details your executor may need. Store this letter in a safe place and update it as needed.

- **Review and Update Your Plan Regularly**: Life changes, such as marriage, divorce, the birth of a child, or the death of a beneficiary, may require updates to your estate plan.
  - ◦ **Action Step**: Set a reminder to review your estate plan every few years or after any major life event. Work with your attorney to make any necessary updates to ensure your plan reflects your current wishes and circumstances.

Conclusion: Building a Legacy That Lasts

Crafting your financial legacy is about more than just passing on wealth; it's about ensuring that your values are reflected in how your assets are distributed and that your loved ones are cared for according to your wishes. By taking the time to plan your estate, reduce taxes and probate costs, engage in charitable giving, and communicate your intentions clearly, you can create a legacy that truly has a lasting impact.

Action Step: Begin by reviewing your current estate plan and identifying any areas that may need improvement. It's essential to work with an estate planning attorney to ensure that your plan is comprehensive, up-to-date, and fully aligned with your wishes. Moreover, communicating your plan to your loved ones is key to ensuring that your legacy is honored in the way you intend.

Estate planning can be complex, and the stakes are high. To ensure your legacy is as secure and impactful as possible, consider scheduling a **Retirement Mastery Consultation** as part of our "**Elite Financial Plan**" package. In this personalized session, our experts will help you fine-tune your estate plan, explore strategies to reduce taxes and probate costs, and provide guidance on charitable giving that aligns with your values. Additionally, you'll receive expert assistance with estate planning, ensuring that your wishes are clearly outlined and legally binding. Together, we'll craft a legacy plan that not only secures your wealth but also reflects the principles and causes you hold dear. See the conclusion of this book for more information on the **Retirement Mastery Consultation.**

CHAPTER 9

Your Path to a Secure Retirement

As you've navigated through the chapters of this book, you've gained valuable insights and strategies to help you secure a financially stable and fulfilling retirement. Let's take a moment to recap the key strategies you've learned, reinforce the importance of proactive planning, and emphasize the need for flexibility in your retirement journey.

This conclusion will also highlight the power of knowledge and expert guidance, encourage continuous learning, and stress the importance of regular plan reviews. Finally, we'll extend a personal invitation to take the next step toward securing your financial future through the **Retirement Mastery Consultation**.

Recap of Key Strategies

Throughout this book, we've covered essential topics and strategies that form the foundation of a secure retirement:

1. **Understanding the Financial Landscape**: Recognizing market trends and their impact on your retirement savings is crucial for making informed investment decisions. By under-

standing past and present market dynamics, you can better navigate the future.

2. **Strategic Retirement Planning**: Balancing growth and stability, adapting to market changes, and protecting your capital are key to maintaining a resilient retirement portfolio. A well-thought-out plan ensures your savings last and continue to support your lifestyle.

3. **Taxes in Retirement**: Managing taxes effectively is vital for maximizing your retirement income. By understanding tax implications, leveraging Roth conversions, and strategically withdrawing from retirement accounts, you can keep more of your hard-earned money.

4. **Insurance Planning**: Insurance is an essential tool for protecting your income, covering healthcare costs, and preserving your assets. Choosing the right insurance products, such as life insurance, disability insurance, and long-term care insurance, can safeguard your financial future.

5. **Key Ages and Milestones**: Recognizing critical milestones, such as when to claim Social Security, enrolling in Medicare, and starting Required Minimum Distributions (RMDs), helps you make timely decisions that optimize your retirement benefits.

6. **Managing Cash Flow**: Creating a retirement budget, establishing reliable income streams, and managing debt are essential for ensuring steady cash flow throughout retirement. Systematic withdrawals and building a cash reserve help maintain financial stability.

7. **Smart Investment Options**: Selecting the right investment vehicles—such as annuities, indexed accounts, structured notes, and dividend-paying stocks—can provide the income, growth, and security needed in retirement.

8.   **Crafting Your Financial Legacy**: Estate planning, reducing taxes and probate costs, and engaging in charitable giving are vital for ensuring your wealth is passed on according to your wishes. Clear communication with your loved ones and professional guidance are key to building a lasting legacy.

The Importance of Proactive Planning

Proactive planning is the cornerstone of a successful retirement. By starting early, you give yourself the best chance to build and protect your wealth, address potential challenges, and make informed decisions that align with your goals. Whether you're just beginning your retirement planning journey or fine-tuning your existing plan, taking action today will pay off in the long run.

Embrace Flexibility and Adaptation in Your Plan

Retirement is not a static phase of life—it's a dynamic journey that requires flexibility and adaptation. As your circumstances, goals, and the economic environment change, your retirement plan must evolve with them. Regularly reviewing and adjusting your plan ensures that it remains relevant and effective, allowing you to navigate unexpected challenges and seize new opportunities.

The Power of Knowledge and Expert Guidance

Knowledge is one of your most powerful tools in retirement planning. By staying informed about financial trends, tax laws, and investment options, you can make better decisions that enhance your financial security. However, you don't have to do it alone. Expert guidance from a financial advisor can provide personalized strategies, help you avoid common pitfalls, and ensure that your plan is aligned with your unique goals.

Encouraging Continuous Learning and Regular Plan Reviews

Retirement planning is an ongoing process that benefits from continuous learning and regular reviews. Financial markets, tax laws, and personal circumstances can change, making it important to stay informed and adaptable. By committing to lifelong learning and regularly revisiting your plan, you can make necessary adjustments and keep your retirement on track.

- **Action Step**: Schedule regular retirement plan reviews with your financial advisor. Consider attending financial seminars, reading up-to-date literature, and staying engaged with financial news to deepen your understanding of retirement planning.

The Importance of Professional Financial Advice

Professional financial advice can make a significant difference in the success of your retirement plan. A qualified financial advisor can help you navigate complex decisions, optimize your investments, and ensure that your plan reflects your goals, risk tolerance, and time horizon. Working with an advisor provides you with the confidence and support needed to make informed decisions and achieve a secure retirement.

Next Steps: Book Your Retirement Mastery Consultation

Now that you've learned the key strategies for a secure retirement, it's time to implement those insights. The **Retirement Mastery Consultation** is your next step toward a confident and secure future.

Personalize Your Retirement Plan with Expert Support

Our **Retirement Mastery Consultation** allows you to work one-on-one with an experienced, licensed financial advisor who will help you tailor your retirement plan to your needs.

Your Path to a Confident Retirement

Throughout this book, you've gained essential insights into the foundations of a secure retirement—from understanding taxes and managing cash flow to choosing the right investments and protecting your legacy. But information alone won't safeguard your future. The true security of retirement comes from one thing: **having a well-crafted, adaptable plan**. Without it, the cost of inaction can quickly erode the future you've worked so hard to build.

The High Cost of Failing to Plan

Without a comprehensive retirement plan, you face significant financial risks:

- **Excessive Taxes**: Every year, retirees leave thousands of dollars on the table by not optimizing their tax strategy. Poorly timed withdrawals and missed Roth conversions can mean paying tens of thousands more in taxes—money that could have stayed in your pocket.
- **Market Vulnerability**: Without a plan, market volatility can decimate your savings, leaving your retirement income

and lifestyle at the mercy of downturns. Without a structured investment strategy, you risk spending down your savings far sooner than anticipated.

- **Healthcare Pitfalls**: Unplanned healthcare expenses are one of the biggest threats to retirement security. Without insurance and long-term care strategies, a major medical event could wipe out a lifetime of savings in a matter of months.
- **Income Shortfalls**: Without planning, retirees often outlive their assets. Mismanaging income sources and ignoring sustainable withdrawal rates can lead to an income gap that leaves you unable to maintain your standard of living in later years.

Altogether, these missed opportunities and unmanaged risks can add up to hundreds of thousands—if not more—in unnecessary costs throughout your retirement. That far outweighs the investment in a structured, expert-guided retirement plan.

Our Three-Step Process to Secure Your Retirement
To help you achieve the confident, well-protected retirement you deserve, we've developed a simple three-step process:

1. **Initial Consultation with a Financial Advisor:** Schedule a meeting with one of our licensed financial advisors to discuss your financial goals and concerns.
2. **Choose Your Plan:** Based on your needs and budget, select a financial planning package that's right for you. Our packages start at an affordable $2,000.
3. **Develop a Personalized Strategy:** Collaborate with your advisor to create a customized financial plan tailored to your specific goals and circumstances.

4.   **Implement and Manage Your Plan:** Your advisor will guide you through implementing your plan's recommendations and provide ongoing support to help you stay on track.

Your Initial Consultation Is Complimentary and Without Obligation: This no-pressure conversation with a licensed financial advisor is designed to help us understand your financial situation and goals. Together, we'll explore whether a financial plan is right for you, and if so, which of our packages best aligns with your needs and objectives.

Retirement Mastery Consultation Financial Plan Packages

1. Comprehensive Financial Plan

This package is ideal for clients seeking a solid foundational plan, including essential services like Roth conversion and financial planning.

- **Roth Conversion Strategy:** Guidance on converting traditional IRA or 401(k) funds to a Roth IRA for future tax benefits while minimizing the tax impact.
- **Financial Planning:** A comprehensive review of income, expenses, savings, retirement goals, and risk management strategies.
- **Retirement Planning:** Building a roadmap to ensure clients' sustainable income throughout retirement.
- **Investment Review:** Analysis of current investment allocations and recommendations for adjustments.
- **Insurance & Risk Management:** Assessing life insurance and other protection needs.

- **Estate Planning Guidance:** Basic guidance ensures beneficiaries and asset transfers align with the client's goals.

2. Advanced Financial Plan

This offering is more suited for clients seeking a deeper, more customized financial planning approach, including stress-testing portfolios, tax strategies, and bespoke solutions.

- **Includes all services from the Comprehensive Plan**, plus:

  - **Portfolio Stress Testing:** Evaluate how the portfolio would perform under different market conditions, helping clients prepare for volatility.
  - **Custom Plan Development:** Highly personalized strategies based on unique financial goals, risk tolerance, and lifestyle preferences.
  - **Tax-Loss Harvesting:** Strategies to minimize tax liabilities by selling underperforming investments at a loss and replacing them with similar assets.
  - **Advanced Tax Planning:** In-depth guidance on managing capital gains, tax deferral strategies, and efficient withdrawal strategies in retirement.
  - **Income Distribution Planning:** Customized plans to manage when and how to draw down assets in retirement while minimizing taxes and ensuring longevity.
  - **Ongoing Support and Adjustments:** As needed, additional reviews and plan updates are provided throughout the year to account for any changes in personal or financial circumstances.

3. Elite Financial Plan

This top-tier offering is designed for clients seeking the most advanced and proactive financial strategies, including estate planning collaboration, multi-generational wealth strategies, and ongoing proactive management.

- **Includes all services from the Advanced Plan**, plus:

  - **Estate Planning Collaboration:** Work closely with estate attorneys and other professionals to ensure a smooth wealth transfer process.
  - **Multi-Generational Wealth Strategies:** Develop strategies for passing wealth to the next generation

Take Action Now for a Secure Future

Your retirement isn't something to gamble on. The cost of **not** having a plan is simply too high to ignore. By scheduling a **Retirement Mastery Consultation** today, you can gain the confidence that comes from knowing your future is secure. With our expert guidance and a tailored strategy, you'll move forward with a clear road map, ensuring that your financial future is protected, resilient, and built to last.

Schedule Your Complimentary Consultation Today, and let us help you realize your retirement goals.

Scan or visit the link below to schedule your complimentary consultation:

MASTERRETIREMENT.TODAY/CONSULTATION

About Retirement Solutions Group

At **Retirement Solutions Group (RSG)**, we understand that retirement is more than just the next phase of life—it's an opportunity to redefine what's possible. Our mission is to empower pre-retirees and retirees with the knowledge, tools, and trusted partnerships they need to build a secure and fulfilling financial future.

Who We Are

Founded by a passionate team of financial educators, publishing experts, and retirement specialists, RSG is dedicated to bridging the gap between complex financial strategies and actionable solutions. We work with a nationwide network of licensed, vetted financial advisors who share our commitment to integrity and personalized service.

What We Do

At RSG, we provide clear, effective guidance on critical aspects of retirement planning:

- **Retirement Income Planning**: Creating sustainable income strategies that provide confidence and stability throughout retirement.
- **Market Protection**: Teaching strategies to safeguard retirement assets against market downturns and volatility.
- **Growth Potential**: Offering insights into competitive, low-risk opportunities for financial growth.
- **Legacy Planning**: Helping retirees preserve wealth and create lasting legacies for loved ones.

How We Educate and Empower

We know the path to retirement confidence begins with understanding. That's why RSG offers a wide range of accessible educational resources, including articles, guides, webinars, and workshops. By simplifying complex financial concepts, we eliminate confusion and replace it with clarity, enabling retirees to take charge of their financial futures.

Our Commitment to You

At RSG, our goal is not just to educate—it's to inspire. We are your partners in navigating the challenges of retirement planning, ensuring that you have the support and guidance needed to make confident, informed decisions.

Why Choose RSG?

- **Trusted Expertise**: Our team brings decades of experience in retirement planning and financial education.
- **Personalized Approach**: We collaborate with a network of advisors who deliver tailored solutions for your unique goals.
- **Accessible Resources**: Every resource we create is designed to simplify the planning process and empower action.
- **Integrity-Driven Guidance**: Transparency and trust are at the heart of everything we do.

With **Retirement Solutions Group**, retirement is no longer a source of anxiety—it's a time of opportunity, freedom, and peace of mind. Let us help you plan for the retirement you deserve with confidence and clarity every step of the way.

Visit us at www.RetirementSolutions.group.